These are the stories of

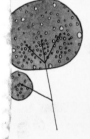

_____

& _____

Date

_____

Just Mom & Me

SHARING OUR LIVES & OUR FAITH

JOURNAL

...inspired by life

EllieClaire.com

*T*his journal is a conversation starter for mothers and daughters. Write what's on your heart: a song, a prayer, a burning question, or a favorite Bible verse. Add lists, pictures, doodles, and fun. How you use it is up to you. It is a gift that is given and received at the same time.

Before the writing starts, you might want to set ground rules like who you can show the journal to, how long each of you can keep it per day or week, and that honest questions/answers will be respected and accepted. It's quite possible the resulting conversations will be equal parts serious, lighthearted, emotional, and spiritual; opening the door to laughter, prayer, and memories for both of you. These pages will build a foundation of trust and love that will be treasured for a lifetime.

Mom

MY FAVORITE THINGS I LIKED TO DO AT YOUR AGE WERE

_____
_____
_____
_____
_____
_____
_____
_____

MY FAVORITE BOOKS WHEN I WAS YOUR AGE WERE

_____
_____
_____
_____
_____
_____

MY FAVORITE SONG WAS

_____
_____

Daughter

MY FAVORITE THINGS TO DO ARE

_____
_____
_____
_____
_____
_____
_____
_____
_____

MY FAVORITE BOOKS ARE

_____
_____
_____
_____
_____
_____
_____
_____
_____

MY FAVORITE SONG IS

_____
_____

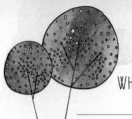

Mom

WHEN I WAS GROWING UP, I WANTED TO BE

_____
_____
_____
_____
_____
_____
_____
_____
_____

BECAUSE

_____
_____
_____
_____
_____
_____
_____
_____
_____
_____

Daughter

WHEN I GROW UP, I WANT TO BE

_____

_____

_____

_____

_____

_____

_____

_____

_____

_____

BECAUSE

_____

_____

_____

_____

_____

_____

_____

_____

_____

Mom

THE THING THAT MOST FRIGHTENS ME

_____

_____

_____

_____

_____

I TRY TO OVERCOME MY FEARS BY

_____

_____

_____

_____

_____

AN ADVENTURE THAT SCARED ME SILLY BUT MAKES FOR A GOOD STORY

_____

_____

_____

_____

_____

_____

Daughter

THE THING THAT MOST FRIGHTENS ME

_____
_____
_____
_____
_____
_____

I TRY TO OVERCOME MY FEARS BY

_____
_____
_____
_____
_____
_____

AN ADVENTURE THAT SCARED ME SILLY BUT MAKES FOR A GOOD STORY

_____
_____
_____
_____
_____
_____

Mom

WHEN I WAS GROWING UP, MY BEST FRIEND WAS

_____

AND HERE'S WHY

_____

_____

_____

_____

_____

_____

_____

_____

WHAT I VALUE MOST IN A GOOD FRIEND

_____

_____

_____

_____

_____

_____

_____

_____

_____

Daughter

MY BEST FRIEND IS

_____

AND HERE'S WHY

_____
_____
_____
_____
_____
_____
_____
_____

WHAT I VALUE MOST IN A GOOD FRIEND

_____
_____
_____
_____
_____
_____
_____
_____
_____
_____

Mom

WHAT I ADMIRE MOST ABOUT YOU

_____
_____
_____
_____
_____
_____
_____
_____
_____

YOU MAKE ME SMILE WHEN

_____
_____
_____
_____
_____
_____
_____
_____

Daughter

WHAT I ADMIRE MOST ABOUT YOU

_____

_____

_____

_____

_____

_____

_____

_____

_____

_____

YOU MAKE ME SMILE WHEN

_____

_____

_____

_____

_____

_____

_____

_____

_____

_____

_____

_____

_____

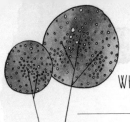

Mom

WHAT I LOVED ABOUT YOUR DAD WHEN WE FIRST MET

_____
_____
_____
_____
_____
_____

OUR STORY BEGAN WHEN

_____
_____
_____
_____
_____

YOU TAKE AFTER YOUR DAD IN YOUR ABILITY TO

_____
_____
_____
_____
_____
_____

Daughter

WHAT I LOVE ABOUT DAD

_____

_____

_____

_____

_____

_____

QUALITIES I WOULD LIKE MY HUSBAND TO HAVE

_____

_____

_____

_____

_____

_____

A TIME I'VE SEEN YOU HELP/SUPPORT DAD THAT I REALLY RESPECT

_____

_____

_____

_____

_____

_____

Mom

MY PRAYER FOR YOU

_____

_____

_____

_____

_____

_____

_____

_____

_____

_____

_____

_____

_____

_____

_____

_____

_____

_____

_____

_____

_____

_____

_____

_____

_____

Daughter

MY PRAYER FOR YOU

_____
_____
_____
_____
_____
_____
_____
_____
_____
_____
_____
_____
_____
_____
_____
_____
_____
_____
_____
_____
_____
_____
_____

Mom

THE ONE WILD, CRAZY THING I WANT TO DO SOMEDAY

_____

_____

_____

_____

_____

_____

_____

_____

_____

_____

_____

_____

_____

_____

_____

_____

_____

_____

_____

Daughter

THE ONE WILD, CRAZY THING I WANT TO DO SOMEDAY

_____

_____

_____

_____

_____

_____

_____

_____

_____

_____

_____

_____

_____

_____

_____

_____

_____

_____

_____

_____

_____

_____

_____

_____

_____

Mom

THE TOP TEN LIST OF WHERE I WOULD LIKE TO TRAVEL AND WHY

1. _____

2. _____

3. _____

4. _____

5. _____

6. _____

7. _____

8. _____

9. _____

10. _____

THE ONE PLACE I HOPE TO NEVER VISIT AGAIN AND WHY

_____

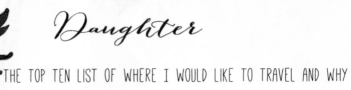

Daughter

THE TOP TEN LIST OF WHERE I WOULD LIKE TO TRAVEL AND WHY

1. _____

2. _____

3. _____

4. _____

5. _____

6. _____

7. _____

8. _____

9. _____

10. _____

THE ONE PLACE I NEVER WANT TO VISIT AND WHY

Mom

DESCRIBE, DRAW, OR ATTACH A PHOTO FROM A MAGAZINE SHOWING WHAT
YOUR DREAM BEDROOM WOULD LOOK LIKE

Daughter

DESCRIBE, DRAW, OR ATTACH A PHOTO FROM A MAGAZINE SHOWING WHAT YOUR DREAM
BEDROOM WOULD LOOK LIKE

_____
_____
_____
_____
_____
_____
_____
_____
_____
_____
_____
_____
_____
_____
_____
_____
_____
_____
_____
_____
_____
_____
_____

Mom

A DECISION I MADE THAT I REGRET

_____

_____

_____

_____

_____

_____

_____

_____

_____

FROM THAT SITUATION, I LEARNED

_____

_____

_____

_____

_____

_____

_____

_____

_____

_____

_____

_____

Daughter

A DECISION I MADE THAT I REGRET

_____
_____
_____
_____
_____
_____
_____
_____
_____

FROM THAT SITUATION, I LEARNED

_____
_____
_____
_____
_____
_____
_____
_____
_____
_____

Mom

THE DAY YOU WERE BORN I REMEMBER

_____

_____

_____

_____

_____

_____

_____

_____

_____

MY FIRST MEMORY OF MY MOTHER

_____

_____

_____

_____

_____

_____

_____

_____

_____

_____

Daughter

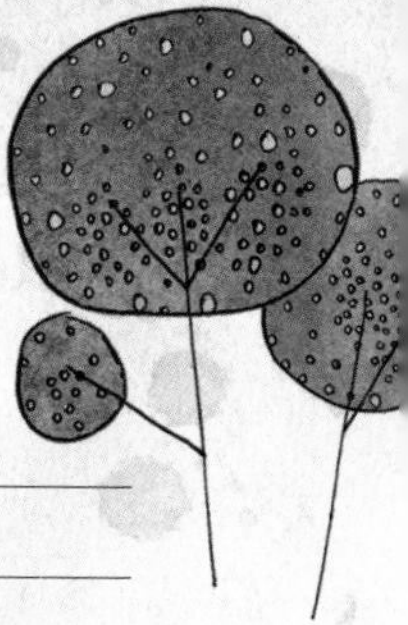

MY FIRST MEMORY OF YOU

MY FIRST MEMORY OF YOUR MOM

Mom

THE MOST REWARDING THING ABOUT BEING YOUR MOM

_____

_____

_____

_____

_____

_____

_____

_____

A CHALLENGING THING ABOUT BEING YOUR MOM

_____

_____

_____

_____

_____

_____

_____

Daughter

THE MOST REWARDING THING ABOUT BEING YOUR DAUGHTER

_____
_____
_____
_____
_____
_____
_____
_____
_____

A CHALLENGING THING ABOUT BEING YOUR DAUGHTER

_____
_____
_____
_____
_____
_____
_____
_____
_____
_____
_____
_____
_____

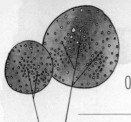

Mom

ONE OF MY MOST EMBARRASSING MOMENTS

_____

_____

_____

_____

_____

_____

_____

_____

I OVERCAME IT BY

_____

_____

_____

_____

_____

_____

_____

_____

_____

_____

_____

_____

Daughter

ONE OF MY MOST EMBARRASSING MOMENTS

_____
_____
_____
_____
_____
_____
_____
_____
_____

I OVERCAME IT BY

_____
_____
_____
_____
_____
_____
_____
_____
_____
_____

Mom

TEN THINGS I LOVE ABOUT YOU

1. _____

_____

2. _____

_____

3. _____

_____

4. _____

_____

5. _____

_____

6. _____

_____

7. _____

_____

8. _____

_____

9. _____

_____

10. _____

_____

Daughter

TEN THINGS I LOVE ABOUT YOU

1. _____

_____

2. _____

_____

3. _____

_____

4. _____

_____

5. _____

_____

6. _____

_____

7. _____

_____

8. _____

_____

9. _____

_____

10. _____

_____

Mom

MY FAVORITE MEMORIES FROM BEING IN CHURCH

_____

_____

_____

_____

_____

_____

_____

_____

_____

_____

_____

_____

_____

_____

_____

_____

_____

_____

_____

_____

_____

_____

Daughter

MY FAVORITE MEMORIES FROM BEING IN CHURCH

_____

_____

_____

_____

_____

_____

_____

_____

_____

_____

_____

_____

_____

_____

_____

_____

_____

_____

_____

_____

_____

_____

_____

_____

Mom

IF I COULD HAVE ANY ANIMAL AS A PET, I WOULD HAVE A

_____

_____

_____

BECAUSE

_____

_____

_____

_____

_____

_____

_____

_____

_____

_____

_____

AND I WOULD NAME IT

_____

_____

Daughter

IF I COULD HAVE ANY ANIMAL AS A PET, I WOULD HAVE A

_____

_____

_____

BECAUSE

_____

_____

_____

_____

_____

_____

_____

_____

_____

_____

_____

_____

_____

AND I WOULD NAME IT

_____

_____

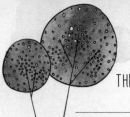

Mom

THE ACCOMPLISHMENT I AM MOST PROUD OF

_____

_____

_____

_____

_____

_____

_____

_____

THE ACCOMPLISHMENT OF YOURS I AM MOST PROUD OF

_____

_____

_____

_____

_____

_____

_____

_____

_____

Daughter

THE ACCOMPLISHMENT I AM MOST PROUD OF

_____
_____
_____
_____
_____
_____
_____
_____
_____
_____

THE ACCOMPLISHMENT OF YOURS I AM MOST PROUD OF

_____
_____
_____
_____
_____
_____
_____
_____
_____

Mom

THE HAPPIEST I'VE EVER FELT (APART FROM WHEN YOU WERE BORN) WAS

_____

_____

_____

_____

_____

_____

_____

_____

MY HAPPY PLACE IS

_____

THE REASON IT MAKES ME HAPPY

_____

_____

_____

_____

_____

_____

_____

_____

_____

Daughter

THE HAPPIEST I'VE EVER FELT WAS

_____

_____

_____

_____

_____

_____

_____

_____

_____

MY HAPPY PLACE IS

_____

THE REASON IT MAKES ME HAPPY

_____

_____

_____

_____

_____

_____

_____

_____

_____

Mom

MY FAVORITE FOOD

_____
_____
_____
_____
_____

MY FAVORITE RESTAURANT

_____
_____
_____
_____

MY FAVORITE MEAL MY MOM MADE FOR ME

_____
_____
_____
_____
_____

Daughter

MY FAVORITE FOOD

_____

_____

_____

_____

_____

MY FAVORITE RESTAURANT

_____

_____

_____

_____

_____

MY FAVORITE MEAL YOU MAKE

_____

_____

_____

_____

_____

_____

Mom

THE BOOK I COULD NOT PUT DOWN

_____

MY TOP TEN LIST OF BOOKS

1. _____

_____

2. _____

_____

3. _____

_____

4. _____

_____

5. _____

_____

6. _____

_____

7. _____

_____

8. _____

_____

9. _____

_____

10. _____

THE BOOK I HATED READING

_____

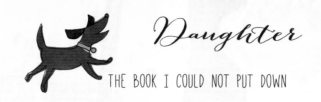

Daughter

THE BOOK I COULD NOT PUT DOWN

MY TOP TEN LIST OF BOOKS

1. _____

_____

2. _____

_____

3. _____

_____

4. _____

_____

5. _____

_____

6. _____

_____

7. _____

_____

8. _____

_____

9. _____

_____

10. _____

THE BOOK I HATED READING

_____

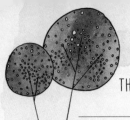

Mom

THE THING I ENJOY ABOUT GOD

_____

_____

_____

_____

_____

_____

_____

_____

THE THING I MOST WANT TO DO/BE FOR GOD THAT SEEMS HARDEST FOR ME

_____

_____

_____

_____

_____

_____

_____

_____

_____

_____

_____

Daughter

THE THING I ENJOY ABOUT GOD

_____

_____

_____

_____

_____

_____

_____

_____

_____

_____

THE THING I MOST WANT TO DO/BE FOR GOD THAT SEEMS HARDEST FOR ME

_____

_____

_____

_____

_____

_____

_____

_____

_____

_____

Mom

WHEN I HAVE FREE TIME, MY FAVORITE THING TO DO

_____

_____

_____

_____

_____

_____

_____

IF I HAD SEVEN DAYS OF FREE TIME AND WOULD NOT BE MISSED BY ANYONE, I WOULD

_____

_____

_____

_____

_____

_____

_____

_____

_____

Daughter

WHEN I HAVE FREE TIME, MY FAVORITE THING TO DO

_____

_____

_____

_____

_____

_____

_____

_____

_____

_____

IF I HAD SEVEN DAYS OF FREE TIME AND WOULD NOT BE MISSED BY ANYONE, I WOULD

_____

_____

_____

_____

_____

_____

_____

_____

_____

_____

_____

Mom

MY FAVORITE HOLIDAY

_____

THE BEST PART IS

_____

_____

_____

_____

_____

_____

_____

MY FAVORITE HOLIDAY TRADITION

_____

_____

_____

_____

_____

_____

_____

Daughter

MY FAVORITE HOLIDAY

_____

THE BEST PART IS

_____
_____
_____
_____
_____
_____
_____
_____

A TRADITION I WANT TO CARRY ON WITH MY KIDS SOMEDAY

_____
_____
_____
_____
_____
_____
_____
_____
_____
_____

Mom

IF I HAD A MILLION DOLLARS, I WOULD

_____
_____
_____
_____
_____
_____
_____
_____
_____
_____
_____
_____
_____
_____
_____
_____
_____
_____
_____

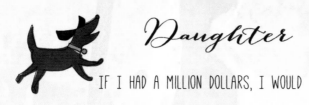

Daughter

IF I HAD A MILLION DOLLARS, I WOULD

_____
_____
_____
_____
_____
_____
_____
_____
_____
_____
_____
_____
_____
_____
_____
_____
_____
_____
_____
_____
_____
_____
_____

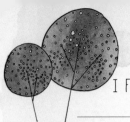

Mom

I FEEL CLOSEST TO GOD WHEN

_____
_____
_____
_____
_____
_____
_____
_____
_____
_____

OVER THE YEARS MY RELATIONSHIP WITH GOD HAS BEEN

_____
_____
_____
_____
_____
_____
_____
_____
_____
_____
_____
_____
_____

Daughter

I FEEL CLOSEST TO GOD WHEN

_____

_____

_____

_____

_____

_____

_____

_____

_____

_____

OVER THE YEARS MY RELATIONSHIP WITH GOD HAS BEEN

_____

_____

_____

_____

_____

_____

_____

_____

_____

Mom

I MAY NOT BE A POET, BUT IF I WAS, I WOULD WRITE ABOUT HOW YOU

_____

_____

_____

_____

_____

_____

_____

_____

_____

_____

_____

_____

_____

_____

_____

_____

_____

_____

_____

_____

_____

_____

_____

Daughter

I MAY NOT BE A POET, BUT IF I WAS, I WOULD WRITE ABOUT HOW YOU

_____

_____

_____

_____

_____

_____

_____

_____

_____

_____

_____

_____

_____

_____

_____

_____

_____

_____

_____

_____

_____

Mom

MY FAVORITE SEASON

_____
_____
_____
_____
_____

WHAT I LIKE TO DO DURING THAT SEASON

_____
_____
_____
_____
_____
_____
_____
_____
_____
_____
_____

THE SEASON I LIKE LEAST

_____
_____
_____

Daughter

MY FAVORITE SEASON

_____

_____

_____

_____

WHAT I LIKE TO DO DURING THAT SEASON

_____

_____

_____

_____

_____

_____

_____

_____

_____

_____

_____

_____

THE SEASON I LIKE LEAST

_____

_____

_____

Mom

IF HEAVEN IS GOING TO BE BETTER THAN ANYTHING WE CAN DREAM,
I IMAGINE IT WILL BE LIKE

_____

_____

_____

_____

_____

_____

_____

_____

_____

_____

_____

_____

_____

_____

_____

Daughter

IF HEAVEN IS GOING TO BE BETTER THAN ANYTHING WE CAN DREAM,
I IMAGINE IT WILL BE LIKE

_____

_____

_____

_____

_____

_____

_____

_____

_____

_____

_____

_____

_____

_____

_____

_____

_____

_____

_____

_____

_____

_____

Mom

IF I COULD HAVE LUNCH WITH ONE PERSON FROM HISTORY, IT WOULD BE

_____

_____

_____

I WOULD ASK

_____

_____

_____

_____

_____

_____

_____

_____

_____

_____

_____

_____

_____

_____

_____

_____

_____

_____

_____

_____

Daughter

IF I COULD HAVE LUNCH WITH ONE PERSON FROM HISTORY, IT WOULD BE

_____

_____

_____

I WOULD ASK

_____

_____

_____

_____

_____

_____

_____

_____

_____

_____

_____

_____

_____

_____

_____

_____

_____

Mom

MY FAVORITE SUBJECT IN SCHOOL

_____

THE SUBJECT I DISLIKED MOST

_____

MY FAVORITE TEACHER

_____

ONE OF MY FAVORITE SCHOOL MEMORIES

_____
_____
_____
_____
_____
_____
_____
_____
_____
_____
_____
_____
_____
_____
_____
_____
_____

Daughter

MY FAVORITE SUBJECT IN SCHOOL

_____

THE SUBJECT I DISLIKE MOST

_____

MY FAVORITE TEACHER

_____

ONE OF MY FAVORITE SCHOOL MEMORIES

_____
_____
_____
_____
_____
_____
_____
_____
_____
_____
_____
_____
_____
_____
_____

Mom

IN MY DAY, SCHOOL WAS LIKE

_____
_____
_____
_____

THE GAMES WE MOST PLAYED

_____
_____
_____
_____

I GOT TEASED ABOUT

_____
_____
_____
_____

SCHOOL BULLYING WAS LIKE

_____
_____
_____
_____

Daughter

FOR ME, SCHOOL IS LIKE

_____

_____

_____

_____

THE SILLY GAMES WE PLAY

_____

_____

_____

_____

I GET TEASED ABOUT

_____

_____

_____

_____

SCHOOL BULLYING TODAY IS LIKE

_____

_____

_____

_____

Mom

IF I COULD CHANGE ONE THING ABOUT MYSELF, IT WOULD BE

_____

_____

_____

_____

_____

_____

_____

_____

_____

_____

_____

_____

_____

_____

_____

_____

_____

Daughter

IF I COULD CHANGE ONE THING ABOUT MYSELF, IT WOULD BE

_____

_____

_____

_____

_____

_____

_____

_____

_____

_____

_____

_____

_____

_____

_____

_____

_____

_____

_____

_____

_____

_____

_____

_____

_____

_____

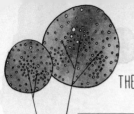

Mom

THESE ARE A FEW OF MY FAVORITE THINGS

_____

_____

_____

_____

_____

_____

_____

_____

_____

_____

_____

_____

_____

_____

_____

_____

_____

_____

_____

_____

_____

_____

Daughter

THESE ARE A FEW OF MY FAVORITE THINGS

Mom

MY DEFINITION OF BEAUTY

_____
_____
_____
_____
_____
_____
_____
_____

I FEEL MOST BEAUTIFUL WHEN

_____
_____
_____
_____
_____
_____
_____
_____
_____
_____

Daughter

THE PEOPLE IN MY LIFE I SEE AS BEAUTIFUL ARE BEAUTIFUL BECAUSE

_____

_____

_____

_____

_____

_____

_____

_____

_____

I FEEL MOST BEAUTIFUL WHEN

_____

_____

_____

_____

_____

_____

_____

_____

_____

Mom

WHEN I'M OVERWHELMED, I USUALLY

Daughter

WHEN I'M OVERWHELMED, I USUALLY

_____

_____

_____

_____

_____

_____

_____

_____

_____

_____

_____

_____

_____

_____

_____

_____

_____

_____

_____

_____

_____

_____

_____

Mom

MY ALL-TIME, MOST FAVORITE MOVIE THAT I'VE WATCHED OVER AND OVER

_____

MY TOP TEN MOVIE LIST

1. _____

_____

2. _____

_____

3. _____

_____

4. _____

_____

5. _____

_____

6. _____

_____

7. _____

_____

8. _____

_____

9. _____

_____

10. _____

THE MOVIE I HOPE TO NEVER HAVE TO SUFFER THROUGH AGAIN

Daughter

MY ALL-TIME, MOST FAVORITE MOVIE THAT I'VE WATCHED OVER AND OVER

_____

MY TOP TEN MOVIE LIST

1. _____
_____

2. _____
_____

3. _____
_____

4. _____
_____

5. _____
_____

6. _____
_____

7. _____
_____

8. _____
_____

9. _____
_____

10. _____
_____

THE MOVIE I HOPE TO NEVER HAVE TO SUFFER THROUGH AGAIN

_____

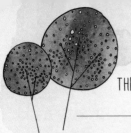

Mom

THE BEST DAY OF MY LIFE WAS

_____

_____

_____

_____

_____

_____

_____

_____

_____

_____

_____

_____

_____

_____

_____

_____

_____

_____

_____

_____

_____

_____

_____

_____

_____

Daughter

THE BEST DAY OF MY LIFE WAS

_____
_____
_____
_____
_____
_____
_____
_____
_____
_____
_____
_____
_____
_____
_____
_____
_____
_____
_____
_____
_____
_____
_____

Mom

THE ONE TIME I THOUGHT, "I WILL NEVER MAKE IT THROUGH THIS DAY" WAS

_____

_____

_____

_____

_____

_____

_____

GOD HELPED ME THROUGH IT BY

_____

_____

_____

_____

_____

_____

_____

_____

_____

_____

_____

_____

_____

_____

_____

Daughter

THE ONE TIME I THOUGHT, "I WILL NEVER MAKE IT THROUGH THIS DAY" WAS

_____

_____

_____

_____

_____

_____

_____

GOD HELPED ME THROUGH IT BY

_____

_____

_____

_____

_____

_____

_____

_____

_____

_____

_____

Mom

I AM THANKFUL FOR

_____

_____

_____

_____

_____

_____

_____

_____

_____

_____

_____

_____

_____

_____

_____

_____

_____

_____

_____

_____

_____

_____

Daughter

I AM THANKFUL FOR

_____

_____

_____

_____

_____

_____

_____

_____

_____

_____

_____

_____

_____

_____

_____

_____

_____

_____

_____

_____

_____

_____

_____

_____

_____

_____

_____

Mom

IF I WAS PRESIDENT, I WOULD

_____
_____
_____
_____
_____
_____
_____
_____
_____
_____
_____
_____
_____
_____
_____
_____
_____
_____
_____
_____

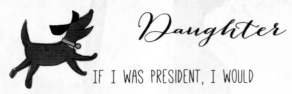

Daughter

IF I WAS PRESIDENT, I WOULD

_____

_____

_____

_____

_____

_____

_____

_____

_____

_____

_____

_____

_____

_____

_____

_____

_____

_____

_____

_____

_____

_____

_____

_____

_____

Mom

SOME GOALS OR ACCOMPLISHMENTS I AM PROUD OF

_____
_____
_____
_____
_____
_____

THE TIME WHEN I WAS PROUDEST OF BEING YOUR MOM

_____
_____
_____
_____
_____
_____

GOALS OR DREAMS I HAVE FOR THE FUTURE

_____
_____
_____
_____
_____
_____
_____
_____

Daughter

SOME GOALS OR ACCOMPLISHMENTS I AM PROUD OF

_____
_____
_____
_____
_____
_____
_____

THE TIME WHEN I WAS PROUDEST OF BEING YOUR DAUGHTER

_____
_____
_____
_____
_____
_____
_____

GOALS OR DREAMS I HAVE FOR THE FUTURE

_____
_____
_____
_____
_____
_____

Mom

SOMETHING PEOPLE TELL ME I AM GOOD AT

_____
_____
_____
_____
_____

SOMETHING I FEEL LIKE I AM GOOD AT

_____
_____
_____
_____
_____

SOMETHING I WISH I WAS BETTER AT

_____
_____
_____
_____
_____
_____

Daughter

SOMETHING PEOPLE TELL ME I AM GOOD AT

_____
_____
_____
_____
_____

SOMETHING I FEEL LIKE I AM GOOD AT

_____
_____
_____
_____
_____

SOMETHING I WISH I WAS BETTER AT

_____
_____
_____
_____
_____
_____

Mom

MY BIGGEST TEMPTATIONS WHEN I WAS YOUR AGE

_____
_____
_____
_____
_____
_____
_____

I OVERCAME TEMPTATION BY

_____
_____
_____
_____
_____
_____
_____
_____
_____

Daughter

MY BIGGEST TEMPTATIONS ARE

_____
_____
_____
_____
_____
_____
_____
_____

I AM TRYING TO OVERCOME TEMPTATION BY

_____
_____
_____
_____
_____
_____
_____
_____
_____
_____
_____
_____
_____

Mom

THE BEST ADVICE I EVER GOT

_____
_____
_____
_____
_____
_____
_____
_____
_____
_____
_____
_____
_____
_____
_____
_____
_____
_____
_____

Daughter

I SOMETIMES WONDER IF YOU EVER WENT THROUGH WHAT I AM
GOING THROUGH. WHEN YOU WERE MY AGE, HOW DID YOU HANDLE

_____

_____

_____

_____

_____

_____

_____

_____

_____

_____

_____

_____

_____

_____

_____

_____

_____

_____

_____

_____

_____

_____

_____

_____

_____

_____

_____

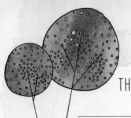

Mom

THE THING ABOUT ME I WISH EVERYONE KNEW

_____

_____

_____

_____

_____

_____

_____

_____

_____

THE THING I WISH EVERYONE KNEW ABOUT YOU

_____

_____

_____

_____

_____

_____

_____

_____

_____

_____

_____

Daughter

THE THING ABOUT ME I WISH EVERYONE KNEW

_____
_____
_____
_____
_____
_____
_____
_____
_____
_____
_____

THE THING I WISH EVERYONE KNEW ABOUT YOU

_____
_____
_____
_____
_____
_____
_____
_____
_____

Mom

I WOULD LIKE TO BE FAMOUS FOR

_____

_____

_____

_____

_____

_____

_____

_____

THE FAMOUS PERSON I MOST ADMIRE AND WHY

_____

_____

_____

_____

_____

_____

_____

_____

_____

_____

_____

Daughter

I WOULD LIKE TO BE FAMOUS FOR

_____

_____

_____

_____

_____

_____

_____

_____

_____

THE FAMOUS PERSON I MOST ADMIRE AND WHY

_____

_____

_____

_____

_____

_____

_____

_____

_____

_____

Mom

IF I COULD SPEND A WHOLE DAY OUTDOORS, I WOULD

_____

_____

_____

_____

_____

_____

_____

_____

_____

_____

_____

_____

_____

_____

_____

_____

_____

_____

_____

Daughter

IF I COULD SPEND A WHOLE DAY OUTDOORS, I WOULD

_____

_____

_____

_____

_____

_____

_____

_____

_____

_____

_____

_____

_____

_____

_____

_____

_____

_____

_____

_____

_____

_____

_____

_____

Mom

MY FIRST JOB WAS

_____

WHAT I LIKED ABOUT IT

_____
_____
_____
_____
_____

WHAT I DISLIKED ABOUT IT

_____
_____
_____
_____
_____

MY DREAM JOB WOULD BE

_____
_____

_____
_____
_____
_____

Daughter

MY FIRST JOB OR CHORE WAS

_____

WHAT I LIKED ABOUT IT

_____
_____
_____
_____
_____

WHAT I DISLIKED ABOUT IT

_____
_____
_____
_____
_____

MY DREAM JOB WOULD BE

_____
_____
_____
_____
_____
_____
_____

Mom

SOMETIMES MY FAITH IS WEAK,
BUT ONE OF THE TIMES IT FELT STRONGEST WAS

_____

_____

_____

_____

_____

_____

_____

_____

THE IMPACT MY FAITH HAS ON MY LIFE

_____

_____

_____

_____

_____

_____

_____

_____

_____

_____

Daughter

SOMETIMES MY FAITH IS WEAK, BUT ONE OF THE TIMES IT FELT STRONGEST WAS

_____

_____

_____

_____

_____

_____

_____

_____

_____

_____

THE IMPACT MY FAITH HAS ON MY LIFE

_____

_____

_____

_____

_____

_____

_____

_____

_____

Mom

SOMETHING I WANT YOU TO UNDERSTAND ABOUT ME

Daughter

SOMETHING I WANT YOU TO UNDERSTAND ABOUT ME

_____

_____

_____

_____

_____

_____

_____

_____

_____

_____

_____

_____

_____

_____

_____

_____

_____

_____

_____

_____

_____

_____

_____

Mom

ONE UNIQUE THING ABOUT OUR FAMILY THAT MAKES ME PROUD

_____
_____
_____
_____
_____
_____

I LOVE WHEN OUR FAMILY

_____
_____
_____
_____
_____
_____

ONE CRAZY THING ABOUT OUR FAMILY THAT SOMETIMES DRIVES ME NUTS

_____
_____
_____
_____
_____
_____

Daughter

ONE UNIQUE THING ABOUT OUR FAMILY THAT MAKES ME PROUD

_____

_____

_____

_____

_____

_____

I LOVE WHEN OUR FAMILY

_____

_____

_____

_____

_____

ONE CRAZY THING ABOUT OUR FAMILY THAT SOMETIMES DRIVES ME NUTS

_____

_____

_____

_____

_____

_____

Mom

MY FAVORITE BIBLE VERSE

_____
_____
_____
_____
_____
_____
_____
_____
_____

A TIME WHEN THAT VERSE REALLY IMPACTED ME

_____
_____
_____
_____
_____
_____
_____
_____
_____

Daughter

MY FAVORITE BIBLE VERSE

_____

_____

_____

_____

_____

_____

_____

_____

_____

A TIME WHEN THAT VERSE REALLY IMPACTED ME

_____

_____

_____

_____

_____

_____

_____

_____

_____

_____

_____

_____

_____

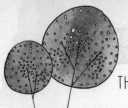

Mom

THE ADVENTURE WITH YOU I'LL ALWAYS REMEMBER

_____

_____

_____

_____

_____

_____

_____

_____

_____

_____

_____

_____

_____

_____

_____

_____

_____

_____

_____

_____

_____

_____

_____

_____

_____

_____

Daughter

THE ADVENTURE WITH YOU I'LL ALWAYS REMEMBER

_____

_____

_____

_____

_____

_____

_____

_____

_____

_____

_____

_____

_____

_____

_____

_____

_____

_____

_____

_____

_____

Mom

I USED TO THINK BEING A MOTHER WOULD BE

_____

_____

_____

_____

_____

_____

_____

_____

_____

WHEN I'M A GRANDMOTHER, I HOPE TO

_____

_____

_____

_____

_____

_____

_____

_____

_____

_____

_____

_____

Daughter

WHEN I'M A MOM, I WANT TO BE LIKE YOU BY BEING/DOING

_____

_____

_____

_____

_____

_____

_____

_____

_____

_____

_____

_____

_____

_____

_____

_____

_____

_____

_____

Mom

THINGS THAT SEEM TO ANNOY ME NO MATTER HOW HARD I TRY TO IGNORE THEM

Daughter

THINGS THAT SEEM TO ANNOY ME NO MATTER HOW HARD I TRY TO IGNORE THEM

Mom

THE MOST DIFFICULT THING I HAVE EVER DONE

_____

_____

_____

_____

_____

_____

_____

_____

_____

_____

_____

_____

_____

_____

_____

_____

_____

_____

_____

_____

_____

Daughter

THE MOST DIFFICULT THING I HAVE EVER DONE

Mom

LIFE'S BIGGEST SURPRISE SO FAR HAS BEEN

Daughter

LIFE'S BIGGEST SURPRISE SO FAR HAS BEEN

_____

_____

_____

_____

_____

_____

_____

_____

_____

_____

_____

_____

_____

_____

_____

_____

_____

_____

_____

_____

_____

_____

_____

Mom

QUOTES I WOULD LIKE TO SHARE WITH YOU

_____
_____
_____
_____
_____
_____
_____
_____
_____
_____
_____
_____

THE QUOTE THAT MEANS THE MOST TO ME

_____
_____
_____
_____
_____

Daughter

QUOTES I WOULD LIKE TO SHARE WITH YOU

_____

_____

_____

_____

_____

_____

_____

_____

_____

_____

_____

_____

_____

_____

THE QUOTE THAT MEANS THE MOST TO ME

_____

_____

_____

_____

_____

Mom

SOMETHING I WANT US DO TOGETHER

_____
_____
_____
_____
_____
_____

THE REASON I THINK IT WILL BE FUN

_____
_____
_____
_____
_____

WHAT I HOPE TO BE ABLE TO DO WITH YOUR KIDS WHEN YOU HAVE THEM

_____
_____
_____
_____
_____
_____

Daughter

SOMETHING I WANT US DO TOGETHER

_____

_____

_____

_____

_____

_____

THE REASON I THINK IT WILL BE FUN

_____

_____

_____

_____

_____

_____

WHAT I HOPE TO BE ABLE TO DO WITH YOU WHEN I HAVE KIDS

_____

_____

_____

_____

_____

_____

_____

Mom

IF I COULD BE ANY PERSON IN THE BIBLE, I WOULD BE

_____

_____

_____

_____

_____

_____

_____

THE BIBLE CHARACTER YOU REMIND ME OF

_____

_____

_____

_____

_____

_____

_____

_____

_____

Daughter

IF I COULD BE ANY PERSON IN THE BIBLE, I WOULD BE

_____
_____
_____
_____
_____
_____
_____
_____
_____
_____

THE BIBLE CHARACTER YOU REMIND ME OF

_____
_____
_____
_____
_____
_____
_____
_____
_____
_____
_____
_____
_____

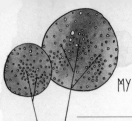

Mom

MY FAVORITE PLACE IN THE WORLD

_____

_____

_____

_____

_____

_____

_____

_____

IT MAKES ME FEEL

_____

_____

_____

_____

_____

_____

_____

_____

_____

_____

_____

Daughter

MY FAVORITE PLACE IN THE WORLD

_____

_____

_____

_____

_____

_____

_____

_____

_____

IT MAKES ME FEEL

_____

_____

_____

_____

_____

_____

_____

_____

_____

_____

_____

Mom

THE ONE THING I'M DOING MY BEST TO STOP NAGGING YOU ABOUT

_____

_____

_____

_____

_____

THE ONE THING I WOULD LIKE TO SEE YOU START DOING

_____

_____

_____

_____

_____

THE THING I LIKE DOING MOST WITH YOU

_____

_____

_____

_____

_____

_____

Daughter

THE ONE THING I AM DOING MY BEST TO STOP COMPLAINING TO YOU ABOUT.

_____
_____
_____
_____
_____
_____

THE ONE THING I WOULD LIKE TO SEE YOU START DOING

_____
_____
_____
_____
_____
_____

THE THING I LIKE DOING MOST WITH YOU

_____
_____
_____
_____
_____
_____
_____

Mom

IN FIVE YEARS, I IMAGINE MYSELF BEING/DOING/HAVING

_____
_____
_____
_____
_____
_____
_____
_____

MY PLAN TO GET THERE

_____
_____
_____
_____
_____
_____
_____
_____
_____
_____

Daughter

IN FIVE YEARS, I IMAGINE MYSELF BEING/DOING/HAVING

_____

_____

_____

_____

_____

_____

_____

_____

MY PLAN TO GET THERE

_____

_____

_____

_____

_____

_____

_____

_____

_____

_____

_____

_____

Mom

THE QUESTION I HAVE ALWAYS WANTED TO ASK IS

_____

_____

_____

_____

_____

_____

_____

_____

_____

_____

_____

_____

_____

_____

_____

_____

_____

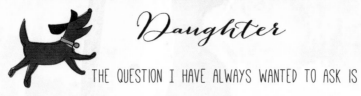

Daughter

THE QUESTION I HAVE ALWAYS WANTED TO ASK IS

_____

_____

_____

_____

_____

_____

_____

_____

_____

_____

_____

_____

_____

_____

_____

_____

_____

_____

_____

_____

_____

_____

_____

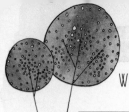

Mom

WHAT I WANT FOR CHRISTMAS/MY BIRTHDAY/JUST BECAUSE

_____
_____
_____
_____
_____
_____
_____

MY FAVORITE KINDS OF PRESENTS ARE

_____
_____
_____
_____
_____

THE PRESENT I ALWAYS WANTED BUT NEVER GOT

_____
_____
_____
_____
_____
_____
_____

Daughter

WHAT I WANT FOR CHRISTMAS/MY BIRTHDAY/JUST BECAUSE

_____

_____

_____

_____

_____

_____

_____

MY FAVORITE KINDS OF PRESENTS ARE

_____

_____

_____

_____

_____

_____

_____

THE PRESENT I ALWAYS WANTED BUT NEVER GOT

_____

_____

_____

_____

_____

_____

Mom

THE SONG I SING LOUDLY WHEN I'M ALONE

_____

_____

_____

_____

_____

_____

_____

MY FAVORITE BANDS/SINGERS

_____

_____

_____

_____

_____

_____

_____

_____

_____

Daughter

THE SONG I SING LOUDLY WHEN I'M ALONE

_____

_____

_____

_____

_____

_____

_____

_____

_____

MY FAVORITE BANDS/SINGERS

_____

_____

_____

_____

_____

_____

_____

_____

_____

_____

_____

_____

Mom

IF I COULD EAT ANYTHING I WANTED FOR BREAKFAST, LUNCH, AND DINNER, MY MENU WOULD BE

_____

_____

_____

_____

_____

_____

_____

_____

_____

_____

_____

_____

_____

_____

_____

_____

_____

_____

_____

_____

Daughter

IF I COULD EAT ANYTHING I WANTED FOR BREAKFAST,
LUNCH, AND DINNER, MY MENU WOULD BE

_____

_____

_____

_____

_____

_____

_____

_____

_____

_____

_____

_____

_____

_____

_____

_____

_____

_____

_____

_____

_____

_____

_____

_____

_____

Mom

ONE OF THE QUIRKY HABITS I LOVE ABOUT YOU

_____

_____

_____

_____

_____

_____

_____

_____

_____

_____

_____

_____

_____

_____

_____

_____

_____

_____

_____

Daughter

ONE OF YOUR QUIRKY HABITS THAT I'M GOING TO TELL MY KIDS ABOUT

_____

_____

_____

_____

_____

_____

_____

_____

_____

_____

_____

_____

_____

_____

_____

_____

_____

_____

_____

_____

_____

_____

_____

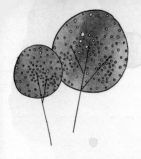

Ellie Claire® Gift & Paper Expressions
Brentwood, TN 37027
EllieClaire.com

Just Mom and Me Journal

ISBN 978-1-60936-953-8

Illustrations by Ellen Matkowski
Typesetting by Jeff Jansen | www.AestheticSoup.net

Printed in China

1 2 3 4 5 6 7 8 9 – 19 18 17 16 15 14